Dear Family,

What's the best way to help your child love reading?

Find good books like this one to share—and read together!

Here are some tips.

●**Take a "picture walk."** Look at all the pictures before you read. Talk about what you see.

●**Take turns.** Read to your child. Ham it up! Use different voices for different characters, and read with feeling! Then listen as your child reads to you, or explains the story in his or her own words.

●**Point out words as you read.** Help your child notice how letters and sounds go together. Point out unusual or difficult words that your child might not know. Talk about those words and what they mean.

●**Ask questions.** Stop to ask questions as you read. For example: "What do you think will happen next?" "How would you feel if that happened to you?"

●**Read every day.** Good stories are worth reading more than once! Read signs, labels, and even cereal boxes with your child. Visit the library to take out more books. And look for other JUST FOR YOU! BOOKS you and your child can share!

The Editors

For my playmates: Robert, Ken, Alexis, and Olivia
—CTB

For my beautiful wife, Nikki,
and my amazing mother, Marilyn.
—MP

Text copyright © 2003 by Christine Taylor-Butler.
Illustrations copyright © 2003 by Mark Page.
Produced for Scholastic by COLOR-BRIDGE BOOKS, LLC, Brooklyn, NY
All rights reserved. Published by SCHOLASTIC INC.
JUST FOR YOU! is a trademark of Scholastic Inc.

ISBN 0-439-56856-0

10 9   08 09 10
                                                                              23
Printed in the U.S.A.
First Scholastic Printing, November 2003

No Boys Allowed!

by Christine Taylor-Butler
Illustrated by Mark Page

JUST FOR YOU!
Level 3

George loved to jump. He jumped to music.
"Cut out that noise!" yelled the neighbors.

He did flips on his bed. "Go outside and burn off some of that energy!" said his mother.

He jumped on the basketball court. "Get lost, Shorty!" teased the older boys.

Poor George. What was a boy to do?

On Monday, George heard a commotion.
A notice was posted at the playground.
Nikki, Kendra, and Jamilla were talking
about it.

"What's that for?" asked George.

"It's for girls," said Jamilla. "Not for boys."

George looked closer. The Playground Rangers were holding a Double Dutch jump-rope contest.

"It doesn't say *girls only*," said George.

"It doesn't have to," said Kendra.
"Everyone knows that jump rope is for
girls."

"What about boxers?" said George,
"and basketball players, and Olympic
athletes, and . . . "

"Well," said Nikki. "I don't think
you are any of those."

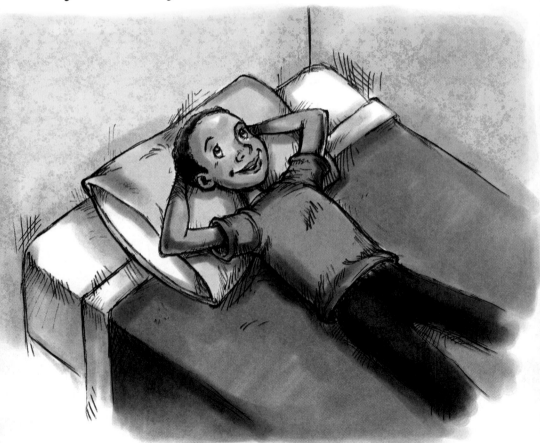

George went home and dreamed
of winning the jump-rope contest.

On Tuesday, George heard a commotion. Two girls were playing on the sidewalk. Jamilla and Kendra turned their ropes in and out, but there was no one to jump inside.

"Tsk-tsk," said George's mom. "It takes three people to jump Double Dutch."

George went outside.

"Can I jump?" he asked.
"No," said Kendra. "Girls only."

So George practiced jumping alone.

On Wednesday, three girls played on the sidewalk. Nikki and Jamilla turned the ropes in and out. Kendra got tangled up in the ropes.

"Tsk-tsk," said George's mom. "It takes a much longer rope to jump Double Dutch." She gave George two long pieces of heavy clothesline.

George went outside. "Can I help?"
asked George.
"No," said Nikki. "Girls only."

George practiced turning by himself.
The playground fence was his turning
partner.

On Thursday, Jamilla and Kendra had much longer ropes, but Nikki got all tangled up.

"Tsk-tsk," said George's mom. "It takes a mighty powerful rhyme to jump Double Dutch."

She whispered her favorite rhyme in George's ear.

When George tried to make a suggestion,
Jamilla, Kendra, and Nikki all said, "Girls
only. No boys allowed!"

So George practiced his jumping rhyme
until he knew it by heart.

On Friday, George stayed inside and practiced all day. That night the playground was empty. George took out his ropes, put on his best jumping shoes, sang his best jump-rope rhymes, and showed his stuff.

His mother and father turned the ropes;
first slowly, then faster and faster. George
didn't miss a beat.

"I think you're ready," said his mother.

"You're going to be great!" said his father.

On Saturday, George heard a commotion.
The playground was full of kids. The
Double Dutch contest had begun.

Jamilla got tangled up in the ropes.
Kendra couldn't remember all the words to
her rhyme. When Nikki jumped in, she
couldn't get out.

Then it was George's turn. He sang his rhyme.

Teddy Bear, Teddy Bear, turn all around.
Teddy Bear, Teddy Bear, touch the ground.
Teddy Bear, Teddy Bear, show your shoe.
Teddy Bear, Teddy Bear, that will do.

George whirled like
a spinning top.

George did a handstand
and wiggled his feet.

George bounced low
and hopped like a frog.

With a flip,
George jumped out
and took a bow.

What a commotion! The crowd went
wild. A Playground Ranger pinned a blue
ribbon on George's chest.

Kendra, Jamilla, and Nikki fumed.

On Sunday, Nikki, Jamilla, and Kendra heard a commotion.

George was on the sidewalk. His mother and father turned the ropes. This time he sang a new rhyme as he waved to the girls.

I like coffee. I like tea,
Come on down and jump with me!

▲▲▲▲▲ JUST FOR YOU ▲▲▲▲▲

Here are some fun things for you to do.

You Can Read **BIG** Words!

The author of this story likes big words! She uses a big word, *commotion*, several times in the story.

▲ Go back and read the story again. As you read, notice the word commotion. Can you figure out what it means from the way it is used in the story?

Here's what the dictionary says: Commotion—Noisy activity.

▲ What are some other words that mean almost the same thing?

How many times can you find the word commotion in this story? ▲

▲ (Answer: commotion is used five times.)

You Can Have **BIG** Dreams!

George dreams about winning the jump-rope contest. Then he works hard to try to make his dream come true.

Do you ever dream about doing something big? Draw a picture about what you can do to make your biggest dream come true. Then make up a story to go with your picture.

▲▲▲▲TOGETHER TIME ▲▲▲▲

Make some time to share ideas about the story with your young reader! Here are some activities you can try. There are no right or wrong answers.

Read It Again: George says two jump-rope rhymes while he is jumping. Read the story again to find George's rhymes. What is your favorite rhyme? Do you know any others?

Talk About: George's parents helped him get ready for the big jump-rope contest. Do you remember a time when a grown-up helped you? Talk about that time. How do you feel when someone helps you do something you really want to do?

Act It Out: George loves to jump! Do you like to jump? Try jumping to music. Try jumping without music. Which do you like best?

Meet the Author

Photo by Van

CHRISTINE TAYLOR-BUTLER says, "Have you ever had something you really wanted to try? But you were too short, or too tall, or too fat? Or you just weren't part of the "in" crowd? That was me. I didn't follow the crowd. I did things that made me happy. Learn to use your special gifts. Practice makes perfect. And one day, when you least expect it, everyone will be cheering for you! I am!"

Christine spent most of her childhood with her head firmly planted in a book. She practically lived in the Cleveland Public Library in Ohio, where she grew up. She graduated from the Massachusetts Institute of Technology, and earned degrees in Art & Design and Civil Engineering. Christine spent 11 years working for Hallmark Cards before becoming an author. She lives in Kansas City, Missouri, with her husband, two daughters, and three cats.

Meet the Artist

MARK PAGE says, "I truly enjoyed working on this book. I guess I could see a little of myself in George. It's no fun being left out when others are having fun. But George didn't get discouraged. He kept doing what he wanted to do. Don't ever let anyone keep you from achieving your dreams!"

Mark graduated from the Art Center College of Design in Pasadena, California; then worked for the Walt Disney Company as a designer. He has always wanted to illustrate for children and this is his first children's book. He lives in Pasadena with his wife, Nikki.